Chefs

Julie Murray

Abdo Kids Junior
is an Imprint of Abdo Kids
abdobooks.com

Abdo
Kids

MY COMMUNITY: JOBS

abdobooks.com

Published by Abdo Kids, a division of ABDO, P.O. Box 398166, Minneapolis, Minnesota 55439.
Copyright © 2021 by Abdo Consulting Group, Inc. International copyrights reserved in all countries.
No part of this book may be reproduced in any form without written permission from the publisher.
Abdo Kids Junior™ is a trademark and logo of Abdo Kids.

Printed in the United States of America, North Mankato, Minnesota.

102020

012021

THIS BOOK CONTAINS
RECYCLED MATERIALS

Photo Credits: Alamy, iStock, Shutterstock

Production Contributors: Teddy Borth, Jennie Forsberg, Grace Hansen

Design Contributors: Candice Keimig, Dorothy Toth

Library of Congress Control Number: 2020910578

Publisher's Cataloging-in-Publication Data

Names: Murray, Julie, author.

Title: Chefs / by Julie Murray

Description: Minneapolis, Minnesota : Abdo Kids, 2021 | Series: My community: jobs | Includes online
    resources and index.

Identifiers: ISBN 9781098205782 (lib. bdg.) | ISBN 9781098206345 (ebook) | ISBN 9781098206628
    (Read-to-Me ebook)

Subjects: LCSH: Cooks--Juvenile literature. | Community life--Juvenile literature. | Occupations--Juvenile
    literature. | Cities and towns--Juvenile literature.

Classification: DDC 641.5023--dc23

Table of Contents

Chefs

Chefs work in kitchens.

They do many things.

Chefs work at many places.

Carl works at a hotel.

Jan is a chef. She works in a restaurant.

Chefs plan the menu.

Arlo makes a list.

11

They train the kitchen staff.

Ellen helps Dan.

They prep the food.

Stan chops carrots.

Ben is a saucier. He makes the sauces!

17

Chefs cook the food.

John uses a big pan.

They put food on the plate.

It looks yummy!

A Chef's Tools

commercial kitchen

ingredients

knife

pots and pans

Glossary

prep
short for prepare, to make ready for a next step.

train
to teach skills.

Index

Abdo Kids
ONLINE
FREE! ONLINE MULTIMEDIA RESOURCES

Visit **abdokids.com**
to access crafts, games,
videos, and more!

Use Abdo Kids code

MCK5782

or scan this QR code!